ALTAMIRA
The Origin of Art

Text:

Dr. Miguel Angel García Guinea

Photographs

Eleonor Domínguez Ramírez

BILBAO
1980

Original Title: ALTAMIRA Principio del Arte
1980 by SILEX ©
ISBN 84-85041-04-6
Depósito Legal: BI-194 - 1980
Imprenta Industrial S. A. Bilbao
(Printed in Spain)

TABLE OF CONTENTS

1.—HISTORY OF THE DISCOVERY OF THE ALTAMIRA PAINTINGS

A.—Discovery of the Cave

The famous Altamira Cave near Santillana del Mar (province of Santander), is considered one of the most treasured monuments of universal art and has become, since its discovery, a mecca for enthusiasts of the history of primitive man or simply of human ingenuity.

As with other great landmarks of man's creativity —the Pyramids, the Acropolis of Athens, the Roman Coliseum and so on— for one who has never been there, Altamira is like one of those persistent longings that spring to life in childhood when on the frontispiece of a school book, one contemplated the silhouettes of bisons then beyond reach.

For those who have had the opportunity of feeling at first hand the impact of Altamira's polychrome ceiling, it marks an unforgettable experience: the glow of humanity in the shadow of an ancient and inaccesible past. There is no sure solution to the mystery of Altamira, but when contemplating the serene gaze of these fiery beasts, one is able to enthusistically exclaim: I have felt the presence of man of 15,000 years ago!

Prehistoric Investigation Prior to the Discovery of Altamira

The discovery of Altamira Cave and the study of its paintings occurred at the dawn of an era of widespread European interest in prehistoric man. There were a few pre-nineteenth-century investigators —more intuitive in their methods than scientific— who took an active interest in man's remote past, and they interpreted certain findings with unexpected foresight. But it was only after 1800 (and in the latter part of the century at that) that scientific investigation began which eventually led to the revelation of that long and timeworn episode in man's history on this planet.

In only 168 years, the almost mythical interpretations of the birth of man and of his culture have given way —aided by the sciences of geology, ethnography, paleonthology, etc.— and the world has been given a fresh and authentic concept of our origin.

The link between geology and prehistory, or one should say the adoption by the latter of geological methodology, in the early nineteenth century, opened a truly scientific path unemcumbered by theological impediments, which has led us to man's remote past — a past until then submerged in dark shadows.

The First Stage: 1800 to 1860

Generally speaking, one can cite two moments in the nineteenth century that signalled the go-ahead for pre-historic investigation. The first period stretches from 1800 to 1860: an heroic time of breakthroughs and battles against certain entrenched beliefs that were graually over-come. A few early pioneers —Gouannet, Tournal, Chris-tol, Schmerling, Picard, etc.— explored caves and brought forth findings that enabled them to verify man's ancient lineage. This led, in 1867, to the publication of a funda-mental work by Perthes ("the individual who captured this communal treasure chest", as Laming called him), entitled "Antiquités celtiques et antediluviennes", in which he establishes beyond doubt the existence of a Quaternary Man.

From 1860 to 1879 (Date of the Discovery of the Paintings)

Working on a base of solid, unquestionable findings, the second stage begins in 1860, and it is a time of heightened emotions for all involved. By 1865, Prehistory has attained the status of a logical and methodical science. It was officially ordained as such in the "First International Convention of Prehistoric Archaeology and Anthropology".

The ever more numerous discoveries —fossils and uten-sils— brought about the structuring of prehistoric science. Prehistoric occupations were now placed in their respective categories. In 1864, Mortillet began publishing "Mate-riaux pour servie à l'histoire primitive de l'homme", and today's system of classification of prehistoric tools is based on his efforts of over a hundred years ago.

Sanz de Sautuola's Research into Prehistory

Such was the state of prehistory in Europe, now raised to an unforeseen scientific level, when Marcelino Sanz de Sautuola of Santander (born in 1851, he was thirty-three years olds when Mortillet initiated the first stage of scientific prehistory) began his purely "amateurish" activities based on clear-minded, modern thinking.

Logically enough, long before his first field-investigations, Sautuola was fully up on all the recent discoveries, and his open-mindedness led him to align himself with the "progressive" thought of his day.

We know for a fact that before the discovery of the Altamira paintings, Sautuola carried out independent studies in several caves throughout the province of Santander.

The Discovery of Altamira Cave

What today constitutes the famous history of Santillana began in the year 1868, when a hunter named Modesto Cubillas Pérez (1) chased after his dog who had gotten trapped between some rocks. He noticed a natural opening in the mountainside and soon spread the news throughout the region of the existence of a cave, until then unknown, in the Juan Mortero district.

The discovery would not have aroused much interest in a land as pock-marked with caves as Santander, had the news not reached the ears of Sautuola. One more cave among the thousands already known would certainly not have interested the local population and the affair might have been quickly forgotten.

Sautuola, who by this time was fully engrossed in the newborn science, received the news from Modesto's co-worker, who was spending the summer in his estate Puente de San Miguel. The proximity of the cave and the knowledge that it might have been sealed for thousands of years prompted Sautuola to investigate.

First View of the Paintings — 1875

We know that in 1875 the illustrious pioneer of Santander's prehistoric studies explored Altamira Cave from top to botom. He himself, in his *Breves apuntes,* described the following experience: "This cave", he writes, "was totally unexplored until a few years ago; I was surely one of its first visitors. At that time, painting number 12 of the fifth gallery already had been sighted. At two feet above the ground, these paintings are clearly visible for their heavy black outlining".

It would seem certain that on this first visit Sautuola placed litle importance on these abstract paintings and probably did not consider them to be the product of prehistoric man. But if nothing else, this anecdote demonstrates his curiosity and scientific temperament. It is quite likely that Sautuola passed over these paintings with indifference, and his exploration would have not acquired any importance, if he had not returned a second time to Altamira.

The Paris World Exposition of 1878

One event in the world of European science —the Paris World Exposition of 1878— was of great importance in Sautuola's professional development. As he himself states, in Paris he had the opportunity of viewing collections of prehistoric objects. He left charged with ambitious projects, which included another visit to Altamira, and he immediately put himself to the task of resuming his research and studies.

B.—Sautuola Sets the Birth of Art Back Thousands of Years

Discovery of the Polychrome Cavern

It is not known in which month or day of 1879 Sautuola returned to Altamira for the second time. On this visit he was accompanied by his nine year-old daughter María. It is likely that this visit, which was to have a lasting effect on prehistoric studies, occured during the summer months.

Still under the spell of those prehistoric objects he saw in Paris, Sautuola returned to Altamira hoping to retrieve fossils, flint, etc., and determined to explored the cave's floor.

Following the light of their carbide lanterns, father and daughter entered the low-roofed bison room and, after thousands of years of oblivion, the little girl suddenly saw on the walls the ocre stains of strange animals forms. (2) There they were —motionless, eternally patient, shrouded in mystery— the famous bisons that today, year after year, attract mass pilgrimages of tourists from all lands.

Astonishment and Doubt

As he himself states, Sautuola was "shocked" upon seeing that marvelous collection of paintings, and he undoubtedly began to wrestle with thoughts and problems that would cause him to vacillate between his intuition and the desire that these were authentic prehistoric paintings, and the doubt that he may be in error. Throughout the pamphlet in which he published his findings in 1880, entitled *Breves apuntes sobre algunos objetos prehistóricos de la provincia de Santander* (Brief Notes on Some Prehistoric Objects in the Province of Santander), we perceive this batle of doubts that must have tormented Sautuola; we also note an increasing certainty on the author's part as to the authenticity of the paintings. His vacillation is evident, for example, in this excerpt: "I am not unaware of the fact that many of my readers may feel that the paintings under study are no more than solace to a modern Apelles; anything is within the realm of possibility. Or in this one: "The highly-developed technique evident in these paintings of the second gallery gives rise to the possibility of their belonging to a later period".

Sautuola Holds Fast to His Belief in the Authenticity of the Paintings

On the other hand, his firm belief and ingenious intuition in ascertaining the origin of the paintings is evident in the following paragraphs:

"Repeated experiments leave no room for doubt that prehistoric man, even when his sole domain was the cave, used to reproduce not only a close likeness of his own figure, but those of familiar animals as well, on elephant bones and tusks; it is therefore not without foundation to assert that if such perfect likenesses were painted on hard surfaces in those days, our cave paintings are also of a similar period.

"One tends to reject the supposition that a more contemporary man might have been so fanciful as to lock himself up in a cave and paint animals unknown to his age".

The very fact that in this pamphlet he reproduced the painted ceiling of Altamira demonstrates the unshakable self-assuredness of a man who exposed himself to the ridicule not only of popular opinion, but of the whole scientific world.

A Prior Consultation With Vilanova?

To launch such a theory on world opinion with the boldness of Sautuola and defend it against all detractors up to his dying day, implies a firm belief in his own judgment— a belief undoubtedly reinforced by another's scientific opinion. In his pamphlet, he considers himself a "mere amateur"... "lacking in formal studies, though not in firm will."

We know that after his first visit to Altamira, Sautuola established contact with Juan de Vilanova y Piera, Professor of Geology at the University of Madrid, to show him the findings of his explorations. Sautuola was already familiar whith his book, *Origen, naturaleza y antigüedad del hombre* (The Origin, Nature and Age of Mankind), published in 1872. (3) Although he makes no mention of having spoken to Vilanova before publication of his *Breves apuntes,* their friendship and the latter's constant support of the theory of the Paleolithic origin of the paintings would suggest a previous interchange of opinions between the two.

Significance of the Discovery of the Paintings

The discovery of Altamira stirred opinion on prehistory in Sautuola's day and opened new and hitherto unimagened inroads into the soul of our most distant ancestors. It can be said that Sautuola's influence on scientific thought of his day caused a wave of shock and disbelief, and later a rapid and revolutionary advance that put within the reach of modern man a living testimonial enabling him to judge the mentality (closer to our own than could have been expected) of prehistoric man. Philosophically speaking, prehistoric investigation enters into deeper waters after 1879. The study of prehistoric man was no longer a theoretical topic; it now began to penetrate the realm of the spirit and being itself. Artistic paths were opened which led back thousands of years into prehistory, thus exposing to ridicule the concept of universal art having originated with ancient Oriental civilizations. The West now claimed almost seven thousand years' seniority in this distinction, which demonstrates an intellectual stature and creativity that now linked us —in our struggles, mishaps, vain hopes and mysteries of life— with that frightened and insecure creature who once attempted to fathom the depths of his spirit and interpret his sensations in man's highest form of self-expression: Art.

Scientific Value of Altamira

The principal scientific value of Altamira is simply this: the discovery and enlargement not just of cold and methodical data, but rather of what was previously known of the awakening of man and his recourse to art to express his deepest anxieties.

The phenomenon of Altamira had and continues to have worldwide repercussions; it surpassed the narrow limits of our knowledge of prehistory and its message reached the four corners of the world. It became a focal point of Western culture and Altamira appeared in textbooks of all nations as the cradle of the History of Art. It was like a rediscovery of America, opening distant and unsuspected horizons in primitive man's intellectual capacity. Sautuola, like a second Columbus, became the first human to intuite, through his passion and hopes, the prehistoric presence of a being endowed with infinite artistic capabilities. In a Darwinist world, Altamira exploded like a bomb, shattering the foundation of a once smug and secure edifice of thought. Darwin's concept of primitive man was erroneously applied to his Paleolithic counterpart. Envisioning a tribe of apes, Darwin compared these cave-dwewers to what he thought must have been our earliest ancestors: "These men", he writes, "were completely naked and painted from head to foot; their long hair was matted and entangled and they bore a savage and defiant countenance. Their artistic production was practicay nil". (4)

If this was the prevailing attitude in 1871, it would have been indeed difficult to imagine man of twelve or fifteen thousand years ago above those tribes of apes.

Prehistoric Man's Creative Capacity

Altamira proved that human groups had evolved spiritually and, in some cases, independently of one another, and on a totally unforeseen scale. The cave-dwellers of Altamira were less removed from modern man than from some of their prehistoric bretheren. The artistic spirit of prehistoric man proved that the germ of human sensitivity could easily take root in minds considered savage from a technical point of view, and that man's creative capacity and the symptom of genius already existed in dawning cultures.

Altamira Transforms the Concept of Primitive Man

After Sautuola, Darwin's concept of primitive beings as applied to prehistoric man was completely transformed. "Those men", we could say, "wore animal skins, their long hair was meticulously cared for, their mouths bore an expression of calm and self-assuredness and their gaze was tranquil, steady and confident. They possessed a perfect sense of art".

Altamira and the paintings that span so many centuries bridge a gap between the first creatures of a developed species and ourselves, who are the last. We could say, as does Teilhard de Chardin, that "what we discover in Altamira is our own infancy; we find ourselves", because we perceive "the same basic aspirations that spring from the bottom of our souls". (5)

C.—Passion and Glory of Sautuola

In 1880, one year after the discovery of Altamira, the appearance of Sautuola's pamphlet, *Breves apuntes,* marks the beginning of a long and bitter struggle against those who mocked the insightful findings of the scholar from from Santander. The struggle extended far beyond the province and across the sea. Year after year, Sautuola had to bear what amounted to an avalanche of disbelief, abuse and open taunts. His very personal honor was put on the line, when malicious rumor accused his house guest, a deaf French painter named Retier, of being the author of the cave paintings.

Prehistory Experts v. Sautuola

It can safely be assumed that when he excitedly came across these paintings, Sautuola never for a moment suspected that they represented a cross he would have to bear until his dying day.

A doubting and accusatory phalanx of the world's foremost scientists closed ranks around Sautuola. How could one seriously consider the authenticity of such supposedly ancient paintings? Was it possible at that time to accept the thesis that primitive man possessed such highly-developed artistic talents, as would have implied the authenticity of the paintings?

How was it that these early prehistorians did not make

the obvious comparison —as did Sautuola— between household art of the period and the newly discovered paintings? In books on Altamira written by foreigners, the attempt was made to excuse the famous French historians who scoffed at the discovery of the paintings, those same who a few years later were made to eat humble pie. Breuil and Obermaier, in their masterpiece on Altamira, state: "Much has been said regarding the bitter opposition that for many years was directed at Sautuola's discovery; although it was unfounded and unjustified, *it can be partially comprehended*. The discovery, which was truly earth-shaking, was something totally unheard of in its day and was considered nothing less than revolutionary. Sautuola opened entirely new vistas, and *it is understandable* that dominant scientific circles would have reacted jealously and negatively". (6)

Obstinacy of the Prehistorians

We agree with the opinion of Breuil and Obermaier in this respect. The news was too shocking, especially in view of Altamira having been the first astonishing find and in spite of subsequent findings. But to give due merit to Sautuola's intuition and deductive talents, it must be asserted that those famous scientists who systematically denied the authenticity of the paintings were wrong— wrong in their unscientific analyses and in their vain and haughty attitude. They refused to recognize the discovery of a figure unknown in the field of prehistory; a unknown, however, whose judgment and confidence in the human value of this new-born science supassed their own. This clearsightedness stemmed more from a heartfelt passion for his field of study and understanding of the life and times of prehistoric man than from a thoroughgoing scientific preparation.

Support from Vilanova

From the outset, as soon as *Breves apuntes* had appeared in print, Sautuola found an implacable ally in the person of his friend Prof. Vilanova y Piera. In the International Congress of Anthropology and Prehistoric Archaeology held in Lisbon the same year that Sautuola's pamphlet appeared, Vilanova passionately defended his friend's beliefs, which were at the same time his own.

Harlé's Report on Altamira

Neither Vilanova's prestige nor Sautuola's enthusiasm could resist the tenacity of Europe's prehistorians. In 1881, the French paleontologist Harlé was sent to Altamira for the purpose of reporting on the controversial paintings. His findings proved negative: he actually believed that they had been painted between Sautuola's two visits to the cave, that is, between 1875 and 1879.

The Rebuttals Continue

From the beginning of the controversy, M. Cartailhac, professor of Prehistory at Toulouse, a respected figure among French scientists, aligned himself with Sautuola's and Vilanova's antagonists, even having never seen the paintings himself. Cartailhac's opinion, along with that of Mortillet —the father of French prehistoric studies— slowly extinguished all hopes of the two Spanish scholars establishing the truth — a truth which no one saw, nor ever bothered to seek.

Opposition in Spain

To further complicate matters, Sautuola and Vilanova also had to suffer the incomprehension of many of their own countrymen. Vilanova worked relentlessly, in speech after speech, to win over the scientists of Spain. In a meeting of the Spanish Natural History Society, on November 3 and again on December 1, 1886 (after six years of struggle!), the matter was brought to the attention of this learned body of men. Eugenio Lemus y Olmo delivered a negative report and added tacitly: "These paintings do not in any way resemble works of art of the Middle Ages, Assyrian, Phoenician or any other ancient period, and at best might be the product of a mediocre modern painter".

Scientific Position of Vilanova and Sautuola

Ever more confident of his position, Vilanova presented a clear, well-thought-out retort that leaves one wondering how it could have failed to convince opposition circles: he established the comparison with the sketches of household articles found in Altamira Cave; like Sautuola, he placed the cave-bed in the Magdalenian period; he brought forth examples of prehistoric paintings that showed "an uncanny instinct and spontaneity" on the part of their authors, in order to check the opinion of those incapable of imagining prehistoric man in possession of such highly-developed artistic skills; he confronted his maligners with common-sense arguments: he inquired of his colleagues of the Spanish Natural History Society if it seemed logical for anyone to go such lengths (as surely the painting of Altamira Cave would have implied) just to put over a hoax.

Sautuola: Pro and Con

His reasoning was all in vain. However, a few less reactionary figures did tend to sympathize with the group of defenders. In Santander, especially, there arose a sort of circle of "Altamira partisans", which included Pérez del Molino, Eduardo de la Pedraja, González Linares, father of Santander's marine biology, etc. These men were opposed by Sautuola's "intellectual enemies", led by the celebrated Santander historian, Angel de los Ríos y Ríos, who showed very litle faith and less knowledge of prehistoric studies. It would have indeed been a task to convince an historian whose opinion was supported by the leading experts of all Europe!

The Truth Springs to the Fore

It was not simple human understanding or reasoning, but prehistoric investigation itself that slowly began to clear the air. The ever-increasing number of finds of household articles in numerous caves throughout Europe

— statuettes, bas-reliefs, carved bones, etc. — pertaining unquestionably to Paleolithic times, coupled with the fossils of extinct beasts, like the mammoth, reindeer, bison, etc., brought the paintings of Altamira ever nearer the world of prehistory. It was now safe to assume that they formed a part of those artistic remmants of primitive man. Scientists such as Piette, Rivière and, finally, Cartailhac, came over to the side of Sautuola and Vilanova.

Sautuola's Posthumous Vindication

Like the paintings themselves, Sautuola's vindication came late. He and his learned comrade had passed away without the satisfaction of witnessing this triumph. Their glory came after death, and perhaps the death of Sautuola was precipitated by the immense burden of sorrow and accusations he was condemned to shoulder. With the discovery of more paintings and carvings after 1895 in the French caves of La Mouthe, Combarelles and Font- de-Gaume, Cartailhac honorably and scientifically rescinded his attack and in 1902 published in "L'Anthropologie" his *Mea culpa d'un sceptique*. This represents an especially significant submission when one considers that Emile Cartailhac represented the most implacable opposition to Sautuola's theory.

Thus the doors of Altamira were finally opened to the wonderment of the entire world. The labors of Sautuola and Vilanova found their rewards. Their disillusionments, sorrows and moments of desperation were now gloriously vindicated - a vindication not just for the departed scholars, but for the theory of prehistory to which they held fast to the end.

2.—ALTAMIRA: «SISTINE CHAPEL OF PREHISTORIC ART»

A.—THE CAVE AND ITS GALLERIES

It is at once odd and ironic that Cartailhac, one of Sautuola's most ferocious opponents, should now bestow upon Altamira the title "Sistine Chapel of Prehistoric Art". It is, however, a name well-taken, and thus Altamira was assured its place in history as man's first spark of artistic activity.

If the idea behind this nickname was to denote two masterpieces painted on ceilings, it is now obvious that the comparison goes much farther. It Michelangelo's Sistine Chapel represents a monumental artistic feat Altamira, whose paintings are twelve or fifteen thousand years older, also symbolizes the highpoint of a culture—the prehistoric era.

The Cave

The cave is 270 meters long and varies in width, narrowing to an almost inaccesible passageway at the end. The entraceway which was blocked until 1868, open onto a large vestibule that for many centuries must have provided shelter for promitive man. Illuminated by daylight, it was an ideal location for many generations of cave-dwellers. The proof is its excavated and still-existent cave bed. Excavations and other work carried out by Sautuola and others in the early part of the century can be observed in the trial pits to the left of the stairs leading down to the cave.

The vestibule leads to the main picture gallery (I on map), the most noted of the cave, whre Paleolithic man left one of the most astonishing and praiseworthy collections of paintings ever. The cave runs through other rooms and passageways (II to IX on the map) to the very end (X), a narrow passage barely two meters wide. There are paintings to be found along the entire stretch.

B.—The Bison Hall

Altamira: One of Humanity's Profoundest and Most Meaningful Achievements

Altamira's fame is based largely on its multicolored bison, horses, wild boar and deer found on the roof of this grotto (see I on map). Given the enormous amount of material published on this topic, it is certainly difficult for us to add anything new, nor shall we try to do so. The dignity, nobility and majesty of these ferocious beasts, their dramatic appearance in the shadowy cavern, their eternal presence, the emission of an unsuspected sensation that they provoke—this can only be felt when standing alone and face to face with these imposing paintings. A touristic excursion to Altamira satisfies one's curiosity, but it can also prove detrimental to one's sense of artistic appreciation. Deep and meaningful things like Altamira should be viewed from a serious contemplative angle. I once remarked that "in the very inalterability of a cave lies the secret of its everlastingness. The cave paintings of Altamira exact more than mere scientific excitement; within, we feel something more human, deeper and decidedly philosophical. Time loses all meaning—it becomes petrified, like a stalagmite. In the darkness, what meaning can the passing years have? In this timeless state, the paintings of prehistoric man awaken a new sense of history, where the distance between generations is miraculously shortened by an extra-historical art. The true and intense emotion of art is felt only when confronted with the original work itself. In the case of prehistoric art, this emotion is intensified even more when we step into the very atmosphere in which it was created. The beauty of stone art lies not only in its technique, nor in the painting itself, but in the surrounding atmosphere—an atmosphere not created by the prehistoric artist but, on the other hand, chosen by him. The dramatic effect of the bisons would have lost much had they been painted on a flat surface. Stone painting must be judged not just by "how" but by "where" as well. Location forms a part of the essence of this art form". (7)

View of the Paleolithic Gallery

The ceiling of this amazing gallery discovered by Sautuola's daughter measures 18 meters in length by 9 across. In prehistoric times, the ceiling was barely two meters above the floor in the central portion and 1.10 meters at the end. (The floor has been lowered to provide access to tourists.) The prehistoric artist found no difficulty in reaching his canvas, but given this short distance, he must of had to have made a great effort —given the dimensions of the paintings (from 1.50 to 2 meters)— to accurately judge the animal's perspective.

Sense of Proportion

In spite of these obstacles, one must admire the instinctive sense of proportion that the early cave-dwellers possessed when we observe how each part of the animals form a harmonious whole. Only the deer displays a somewhat off-balanced shape, though not so when the angle of view of its creator is taken into account. From the lowered floor, we can today take in a panorama that primitive man could only appreciate lying down.

The Bison

The animal that appears with most frequency is the bison (16 paintings). Some are especially striking for assuming the form of rocky moles on the ceiling, thus combining the double effect of color and form. Of the most outstanding are those standing bison, eleven in all, including one running and another headless one, or those depicted in tense poses, hunched, ready to spring forward or looking backward in expectant anxiety. No cave known to us offers such a variety of bison paintings; it is as though the artist had wanted to display every imaginable facet of this beast's dynamism.

Other Animals in the Gallery

Aside from several other lesser artistic manifestations, the collection is completed by paintings of horses, deer —the largest of all the figures (2.25 meters)— and so on. They are especially interesting for having been cut, as well as painted onto the rock.

The Mysterious Meaning of the Paintings

What strange force compelled prehistoric man to assemble this collection of souvenirs of what was his main daily concern—the hunt? Was the bison at the point of extinction, or in migration, and would this then have been a symbol of his desire to recapture the presence of this coveted animal? Was the bison man's mystic symbol of the mystery of life? Was the cave a center of religious rites or of a nascent mythology? In spite of much theorizing, nothing certain can be said regarding the significance of these paintings. There is an unknown relationship between the hunt, magic, mystery and rite, but we are ignorant of whatever primitive mental process may have tranformed metaphysical or practical anxiety into art.

Reality or Illusion? — Religious Art

This collection of animal paintings makes the legacy of Altamira the most clear-cut example of primitive emotion. A solitary figure painted somewhere on a wall would always have a less dramatic and overwhelming appearance. The repetition of figures on a wall produces an effect of animate life. There they are, shuffling their paws, bowing their heads, twisting their manes or galloping across the fields. We do not see the animals: what we do see is the essence of the species, transformed by man into myth and religious ritual. Rock painting is charged with an almost unbelievable quality of mystery. We see not reality (although it has often been interpreted in this manner) but illusion. The animal paintings of prehistoric man are ponderous and impressive —it is by no means a childish or elementary phenomenon— and full of religious force. They can confidently be placed within the category of man's first religious art form.

The paintings of Altamira and Niaux defy judgment by esthetic standards; they must be viewed and appraised philosophically. They are the most beautiful fossils belonging to that heroic episode in the formation of the human spirit and of man's struggles with forces unknown to him.

The mystery of these paintings, anchored in time as they are, is the very mystery of man confronted with a force beyond his grasp. The great ceiling of Altamira is like an eternal sigh or life —a longing to feel and express— a sigh heaved by a primitive man nostalgically aware of his impotence.

C.—Other Carvings and Paintings in the Cave

Altamira is not Only the Cave of the Bison

If this Wagnerian symphony of prehistoric art resounds throughout the great polychrome gallery, other less boisterous melodies are also to be heard from other parts of the cave. (8)

Relation to Other Carvings and Paintings

If we follow the galleries and passageways, we find on the walls and ceiling a copious arrangement of carvings and paintings.

In Passageway II on the map, in the clay-like spongy cavern, we see a finger-painted decoration which takes the form of an ox and other "macarroni" shapes (No. 1 on map).

In Hall III, in the brace of stalagmites to the left, there is what appaears to be the headless form of a horse (No. 2 on map).

Following the outline of the rock, on the opposite wall, there are some paintings of horses, deer and, finally, a group of reddish linear designs (No. 2 on map.)

In number 4 on the map there is a cornise containing a deer painting. On the other wall, in the passage between, Hall III and Corridor IV, there are several etchings of deer, in some places superimposed on one another (No. 5 on map).

In Gallery V (No. 6) there is a bull carved on a cornise and below, on the cave wall, what appears to be a horse painted in black. In this same gallery, in number 7, there is a well-preserved black bison.

To the left of the inner part of Hall VI there are black paintings of a deer and three mountain goats (No. 8 on map). In number 9 of the same gallery, a beautiful medium-size bull in black stands out.

In Hall VIII there are various carved designs of no special note.

There are numerous interesting figures all along the narrow tail end of Gallery X on the map.

Throughout this section of the cave there are finely-painted bison, deer heads, animated horses and oxen as well as sketchy drawings denoting a hastily improvised impression. Lastly we find abstract occult symbols akin to the most advanced techniques of the modern school of art.

Altamira represents more than its famous room of bison paintings; it is an extraordinary complex of lesser carvings and paintings spread across the entire length of the cave. If Breuil's chronological classification were not so open to debate (as well as the theory which aims to replace it), we could assert that this cave is the finest example of prehistoric man's artistic creation and evolution, from the simplest line drawings to the majestic multi-colored finale. Thousands of years of humanity and the artistic advance of man are enclosed within the walls of Altamira Cave.

D.—Artistic Value of Altamira Paintings

Masterpiece of the Era

The scientific value of this discovery is self-evident: it bridged the gap between us and that unknown mentality of Western man and the culture of his time. Breuil and Obermaier, in their famous book said: "Almost every imaginable question posed to an art which had reached its zenith has found its reply in Altamira: the real depiction of form, its shaping with the aid of blended colors or delicately-contrasted tones, done in such a way as to highlight light and shadow, the sensation of movement, etc.". (9)

Professor Pericot singles out the everlasting value of the paintings of Altamira: "In beauty and antiquity these paintings have no equal. In Altamira, painting reached an insuperable height which can only be copied in other subject matter and form... they represent a primitive though mature art and are proof of the similarity of ancient man's mentality to our own—an extraordinary intelligence, the divine spark that separates man from matter". (10)

Within the panorama of prehistoric painting —including the amazing discoveries of Lascaux— Altamira stands alone, not only for being the first, but also the one which defies artistic comparison. It would be difficult indeed to contest this primacy. It is true that we still have no idea of what the earth's entrails hold in secret regarding its ancient inhabitants. Many caves inhabited thousands of years ago must still be sealed, as were Altamira and Lascaux. But today, and perhaps forever, Altamira is the mecca of those who seek to contemplate these stirring bisons and who wish to enter, as Teilhard de Chardin has said, "the reflexive and overflowing consciousness of these forgowtten being...", "when we perceive in the artists of this far-off era... the perfection of movement and those silhouettes, the spontaneity of the ornamental reliefs, the sense, of observation, the fancy of joy and of creation". (11)

E.—The Archeological Deposits of Altamira

Sautuola Excavates the Cave

If Altamira's historical importance is owed exclusively to the path it opened in man's spiritual awareness, no less important are the inroads into the understanding of prehistoric man's daily life. When in 1875 Sautuola first entered the cave, he did so with the purpose of discovering concrete traces of primitive man. As he says in *Breves apuntes,* that year, as in 1879 —the year of the great discovery— he found a sizeable quantity of carved flint and sharpened bones that could only have been fashioned by human hands. Sautuola realized the importance of this find and he maintained steady contact with Vilanova who donated a collection of similar finds. A part of these objects reached the public eye in *Breves apuntes* in the form of sketches possibly of Sautuola's own hand. There are large slice of flint of the Magdalenian period, some plain and others carved, sharp tips, stone chips, deer teeth, bone picks and spears, some decorated with lines, bone needles, stone plaques like barnacles, pendents, etc.

Early Explorations in the Cantabrian Region

Aside from opening the way to the discovery of prehistoric painting, Sautuola initiated the first Paleolithic excavations in the Cantabrian region which in time became the focal point (along with Dordogne and Ariêge) for the study of prehistoric man.

Other Explorers

After Sautuola's first visit to Altamira, others carried out their own studies of the cave — E. de la Pedraja, Vilanova, Harlé and also Cartailhac and Breuil.

Interesting Excavations of Alcalde del Río

Alcalde del Río, the discoverer of Castillo Cave in Puente Viesgo, undertook investigations in the cave and established two geological levels: a higher period of the Magdalenian era (coal-like) and a lower period (clay-like). The discoverey of this level of bones engraved with bison and deer, in excellent condition, has put Brueil's chronology theory, and even that of the pictures themselves, in jeopardy. Professor Jordá has now taken up this problem of chronology, in spite of the systematic efforts of Leroi-Gourhan (12).

Obermaier's Excavations
How Old Are the Paintings?

Later explorations in Altamira were carried out by Obermaier in 1924 and 1925. He found the same two levels as Alcalde del Río and even discovered "red and yellow ocre pencils of different shapes, wood carbon and grayish-white loam representing the materials used for blending colors". He also found red, yellow or grayish-white clay. This fact, coupled with the absence of a higher Magdalenian period in Altamira, would put the dating of the pictures of this period much in doubt, which brings up he possibility of an even earlier origin. The debate is already underway.

FOOTNOTES

(1) Fr. María Patricio Guerin: *El centenario del descubrimiento de la cueva de Altamira*, «Altamira», nos. 1, 2, 3, 1967, pps. 141-146.

(2) The cry she was believed to have uttered, «Look, daddy, bulls!», has been corrected by her son Emilio Botín S. de Sautuola, to «Look, daddy, oxen!». This is logical, since in those days, oxen were used for farming in Santander.

(3) See P. Jesús Carballo: *M. S. de Sautuola. Antología de escritores y artistas montañeses*, XIV, 1950. Santander, p. XXXVII.

(4) Charles Darwin: «The Origin of Species».

(5) Teilhard de Chardin: *El fenómeno humano*, «Revista de Occidente», 1958, p. 204.

(6) H. Vreuil and H. Obermaier: *La Cueva de Altamira de Santillana del Mar*, Madrid, 1935, p. 6.

(7) M. A. García Guinea: Bulletin of the «Société Prehistorique de l'Ariège», vol. XVIII, 1963, p. 6.

(8) The standard work on the paintings of Altamira is that compiled With the cooperation of the *Junta de las Cuevas de Altamira*, the Hispanic Society of America and the Spanish Academy of History, published in Madrid in 1935. Its title (already mentioned in note 6) is «La Cueva de Altamira en Santillana del Mar» and its authors the abbey Breuil and Dr. Hugo Obermaier, who painstakingly undertook the task of analyzing, copying and describing in detail every painting in the Cave.

(9) H. Breuil amd H. Obermaier: *op. cit.*, p. 12.

(10) L. Pericot: *Sobre el arte rupestre cantábrico*. Address on the innaguration of the academic year at the Universidad Internacional Menéndez y Pelayo, Santander, 1953, p. 25

(11) Teilhard de Cardin: *El fenómeno humano*, «Revista de Occidente», 1958, p. 205.

(12) A. Leroi-Gourdan: *Préhistoire de l'art occidental*, París, 1965.

BIBLIOGRAPHY OF THE ALTAMIRA CAVE

RODRIGUEZ FERRER, M.: «Apuntes de un diario.» *La Ilustración Española y Americana.* 1879.

SAUTUOLA, M. de: *Breves Apuntes sobre algunos objetos prehistóricos de la provincia de Santander.* Santander. 1880.

VILANOVA Y PIERA: *Sur la Caverne de Santillana.* A. F. A. S. 1881, pág. 765 y 1882, pág. 89-93. *La gruta de Altamira.* Actas de la Sociedad Española de Historia Natural, 1886.

CARTAILHAC, E.: «Les cavernes ornées de dessins, La Grotte d'Altamira» (Espagne), «Mea culpa d'un sceptique». *L'Anthropologie.* 1902.

ALCALDE DEL RIO, H.: *Pinturas y grabados de las cavernas de Santander.* Santander. 1906.

CARTAILHAC, E. y BREUIL, H.: *La caverne d'Altamira à Santillana près de Santander (Espagne).* Mónaco. 1906.

ALCALDE DEL RIO, H., BREUIL, H. y SIERRA, L.: *Les cavernes de la région cantabrique.* Mónaco. 1911.

CABRE AGUILO, J.: *El arte rupestre en España.* Comisión de Investigaciones Paleontológicas y Prehistóricas. Madrid. 1915.

OBERMAIER, H.: *Las cuevas de Altamira.* Patronato Nacional de Turismo. 1928.

— *Altamira.* IV Congreso International de Arqueología (en alemán). 1929.

BREUIL, H. y OBERMAIER, H.: *The Cave of Altamira at Santillana del Mar (Spain).* Madrid. 1935; edic. española. 1935.

CARBALLO, J.: *Descubrimiento de la cueva y pinturas de Altamira por don Marcelino de Sautuola.* Patronato de las Cuevas Prehistóricas. Santander. 1950.

— *La cueva de Altamira y otras cuevas pintadas en la provincia de Santander.* Patronato de las Cuevas Prehistóricas. 1950. 2.ª edic. 1956.

MAZA SOLANO, T.: «Notas para la bibliografía de la cueva de Altamira.» *Altamira.* 1950. Núms. 1 y 2, pág. 92.

BREUIL, H.: *Quatre cents siècles d'art pariétal.* Montignac. 1952.

GRAZIOSI, P.: *L'arte dell' antica Etá della Pietra.* Florencia. 1956.

LEROI - GOURHAN, A.: *Préhistoire de l'art occidental.* París. 1965.

LIST OF BLACK AND WHITE PLATES

PLATE 1

Marcelino Sanz de Sautuola (1831-1888), discoverer, along with his daughter María, of the Altamira paintings (1879). He defended their authenticity against nearly entire scientific world of his day.

PLATE 2

María Sanz de Sautuola, approximately at the age when she saw the «oxen» of Altamira for the first time.

PLATE 3

Facsimile of the cover of the pamphlet published by Sautuola in 1880 in which he defends his belief in the Paleolithic origin of the paintings.

PLATES 4 AND 5

First copy of the Altamira paintings published by Sautuola in *Breves apuntes* in 1880.

PLATES 6 AND 7

General layout of Altamira Cave. The hall marked «1» is the famous polychrome bison hall.

PLATE 8

A deer 66 cms. long engraved on the ceiling of the gallery of paintings. It is near several reddish horses at the bottom right.

PLATE 9

A group of black symbols to the left of gallery No. 10.

PLATE 10

Laurel, willow and grooved leaves from Altamira's Magdalenian period. (Excavations of H. Alcalde del Río. Museum of Prehistory of Santander.)

PLATE 11

Engraving of a deer located on the wall in the spot indicated by No. 4 on the map.

PLATE 12

Deer carvings on the shoulder blades of another deer, discovered during the explorations of Alcalde del Río.

PLATE 13

Above: black bison, located in Hall VI, at N.º 9 on map. Below: bison carving on the right wall of the last passageway, marked No. X on map.

PLATES 14 AND 15

Altamira in the province of Santander. From the provincial capital, take the Oviedo road. At Barreda, detour toward Santillana del Mar and from there, direct to the caves.

PLATE 16

Human-like carvings in the gallery of paintings.

LIST OF COLOR PLATES

PLATE 1

Head of a bull or bison, in black, approximately in the center of the polychome hall. Here the prehistoric artist has achieved a beautiful contour drawing reduced to its simplest and most expressive lines. The proportions, the animation, the bold lines and even the human-like gaze offer a vivid example of the artistic and creative capacity of the cave-dweller.

PLATES 2 AND 3

A general view of part of the multicolored ceiling. In the foreground, the hunched bisons. Their position, on the natural contour of the rock, enhances and highlights their proportions. To the left we find two other bisons: one hunched over and the other erect. In Altamira, color art acquires its greatest height of beauty. Prevailing tones are ocre and black; the former was used mostly for shading and the latter for outlining the body and most important parts of the animals, such as hooves, tail, head, name, etc. Materials used for painting were drawn directrly from Nature and were mixed with animal grease, thus producing a primitive sort of watercolor. Black was produced from charcoal; red, yellow and brown hues from ruddy earth and hematite; the delicate touches of purple were derived from manganese. The ceiling of the hall of paintings is approximately 18 meters long and 8 or 9 meters wide and contains over thirty animal figures covering the central section of the cave.

PLATES 4 AND 5

A bison in running or jumping position. The head is visible near the upper left-hand corner and one can clearly make out the black, almost horizontal horn. Alongside is the etching of the eye. The nape and loins are deeply outlined in black. The thick front hooves, also outlined in black, point down to the left an there are carved lines that follow the direction of the painting. The belly and hind hooves are shaded in black. Since Breuil's first copies of the paintings in 1932, there has been no noticeable deterioration in their coloring. In his book, Breuil stated that some had appeared to have faded since his first works were carried out in 1902. All technological means are now being employed to insure the preservation of these paintings in their original state. Is is known, for example, that there is a varying range of humidity within the cave according to the month of the year and external conditions. When the humidity reaches its peak —97 degrees— the paintings acquire their most brilliant coloring, while when it dips to 94 degrees, usually in August, the colors begin to fade.

PLATES 6 AND 7

A motionless, erect bison. The torso of this bison, like many figures in the cave, is to a large extent carved in the rock: horns, eye, snout, legs and name. This figure is surrounded by a headless, standing bison (its tail is visible in the lower right-hand corner) and a sleeping bison (a fragment is shown in the lower left-hand corner) and a bellowing bison.

PLATES 8 AND 9

A large multicolored bison with its tail raised. It is over two meters long. Somewhat isolated from the rest, it is an enormously attractive figure. It is the classic bison repeated over and over again in Altamira. Its face, which appears bearded, assumes a human and almost Assyrian semblance. Nearby, there are reddish colored symbolis. The only carved portions are the nape, the eye and the horns, part of the hind hoof, the belly and part of the hind quarters.

PLATES 10 AND 11

A headless bison and front quarters of the standing bison of plates 6 and 7. This painting is 1.50 meters long. There are no signs to indicate that the prehistoric artist ever intended to paint the head. On the other hand, there is good reason to believe that this headless beast served some mystical or religious purpose, but we do not yet have sufficient data on prehistoric painting to draw any concrete conclusions. Many varied and well-founded theories have arisen around these paintings: from totemism, ancestor worship, fertility rites, magic, etc., to the most recent of Leroi-Gourhan, who believes that painted caves represent sanctuaries of a primitive cult based on a mythology of opposing male and female forces.

PLATES 12 AND 13

A crouching female bison. Painted on a prominent bulge in the cave wall. It is one of the most expressive and admirable paintings of Altamira. The artist has cleverly adapted the figure of the bison to the natural contour of the rock; its head is forced downward, its legs doubled, and it displays a freedom of movement unencumbered by rules of style —rigidity and fixed posture— of traditional schools of religious art. The posture of animals in prehistoric art is never bound by restrictions of style; thus we find an abundant variety of side views throughout the cave.

PLATES 14 AND 15

A large standing female bison, looking to the right, placed between the black bull or bison head of Plate 1 and one of the crouching bisons. Its exact position on the ceiling can be seen in the foreground of Plates 2 and 3. The colors are very well-preserved and some of the more important parts of the body are engraved: head, forelegs and one hind leg.

PLATE 16

Detail of preceding Plate: forelegs of female bison. Vertical engraved lines can be faintly seen surrounding the painting. The double technique of painting and engraving was a normal procedure in prehistoric art, not only at Altamira but also in many other Spanish and French caves. The most representative drawings in this respect are to be seen here and at Font de Gaume in France. There are large multicolored figures at Tito Bustillo Cave in Ribadesella (discovered in 1958), above all reindeer and horses, where the same technique of engraving or chiseling is used to outline the paintings.

PLATE 17

Detail of Plates 14 and 15; head of female bison.

PLATES 18 AND 19

A group of bison from the polychrome ceiling. The standing bison of Plates 6 and 7 and the crouching bison of Plates 12 and 13 can be seen in their entirety. This fragment shows that there was no prearranged order; the animals seem to adapt themselves to any available space on the rock surface.

PLATES 20 AND 21

A crouching bison looking backward. Above is a bellowing bison. The engraved legs of the latter are in a horizontal position in the middle and to the top of the photograph. These two active bison, in expressive Baroque positions, give us a good idea of the advanced technique of the Altamira Cave artists.

PLATES 22 AND 23

A magnificent huge deer, 2.25 meters long, facing right; it is the largest in the cave. Paintings at Tito Bustillo Cave in Ribadesella compete in dimensions with the Altamira animals and even surpass them where reindeer are concerned. Another deer at Tito Bustillo is an exact replica in size and posture of this Altamira deer. These gigantic animals are further living proof of the advanced artistic technique of Paleolithic man.

PLATE 24

Detail of Plates 22 and 23: head of deer. Eye, muzzle, ears and contours of head are all engraved.

PLATE 25

Detail of Plates 22 and 23: head, neck and forelegs of deer. The exceedingly thin legs are set apart and engraved at the top. There is a small black bison painted underneath the neck of the deer.

PLATES 26 AND 27

An ocre horse on the left edge of the wall. Within the figure of the horse, and probably painted at an earlier date, can be seen a deer slightly more reddish in color (almost invisible on the photograph). The head is pointing downward and is located where the forelegs of the horse join. This is a kind of pony which Breuil considers to be one of the oldest paintings on the ceiling. Similar horses can be seen at Ribadesella.

PLATES 28 AND 29

Detail of Plates 12 and 13: mid-section of the crouching or leaping bison. The beginning of a black horn and an eye can be seen at the bottom left-hand corner. To the right, the forelegs are doubled up. Note the quality of the limestone which is perforated in places and cracked. Howerer, there does not seem to be any inmediate danger of collapse. The *Patronato de las Cuevas Prehistóricas* of the province of Santander, in charge of all caves containing prehistoric art, remains constantly on the alert.

PLATES 30 AND 31

A standing bison, slightly apart from the others, at the entrance to the polychrome hall. The contours are rather vague but the animal has been profusely engraved. There is slight engraving (visible on the photograph) around the eye, muzzle and whiskers.

PLATE 32

Designs painted in red near the deer in Plates 22 and 23. To the top of the photograph and to the right is the little black bison painted underneath the neck of the deer. These abstract figures have been given various interpretations; the most widely accepted theory is that of Leroi-Gourhan, who considers them to be female symbols.

PLATE 1

PLATE 2

BREVES APUNTES

SOBRE

ALGUNOS OBJETOS PREHISTÓRICOS

DE LA

PROVINCIA DE SANTANDER,

por

DON MARCELINO S. DE SAUTUOLA,

C. de la Real Academia de la Historia.

SANTANDER, 1880.

Imp. y lit. de Telesforo Martinez,
BLANCA, 40.

PLATE 3

PLATES 4 AND 5

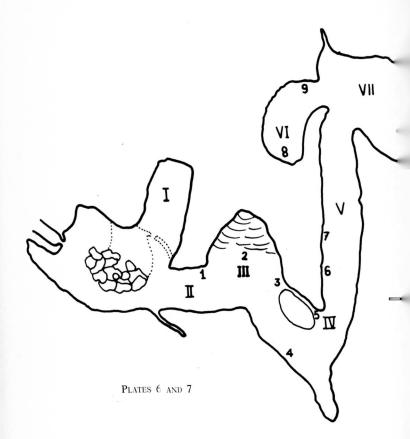

PLATES 6 AND 7

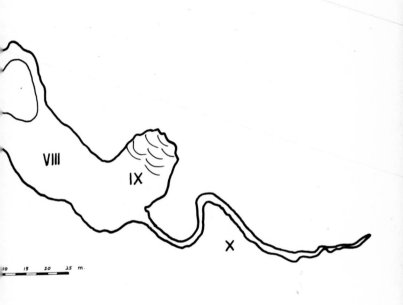

PLATE 8

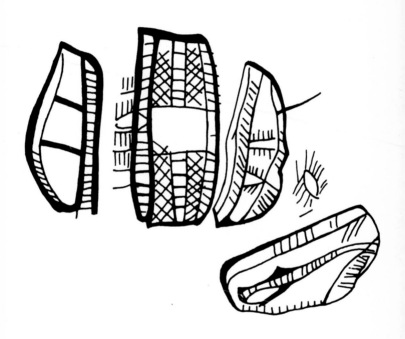

PLATE 9

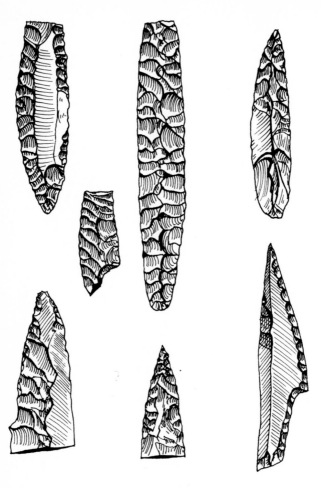

PLATE 10

PLATE 11

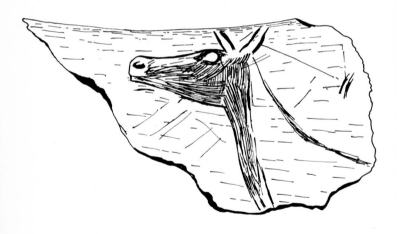

PLATE 12

PLATE 13

ASTURIAS

Cra. Santander- Oviedo

ALTAM

Torrelavega

Reinosa

PALENCIA

SANTANDER

Castro
Urdiales

VIZCAYA

BURGOS

PLATES 14 AND 15

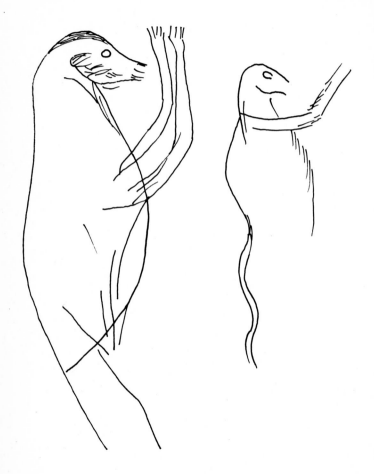

PLATE 16

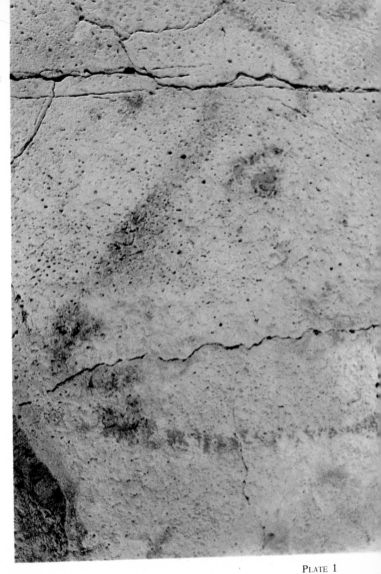

PLATE 1

PLATES 2 AND 3

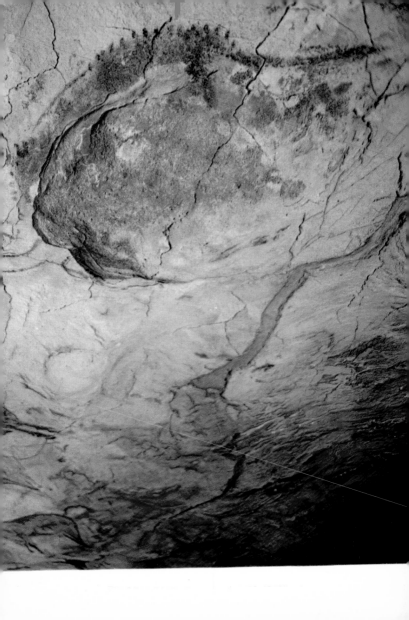

PLATES 4 AND 5

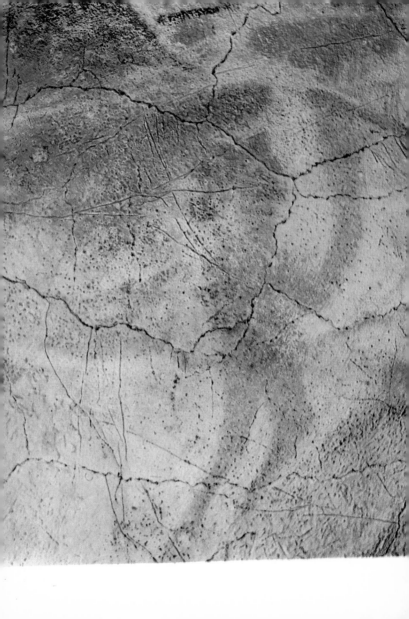

PLATES 6 AND 7

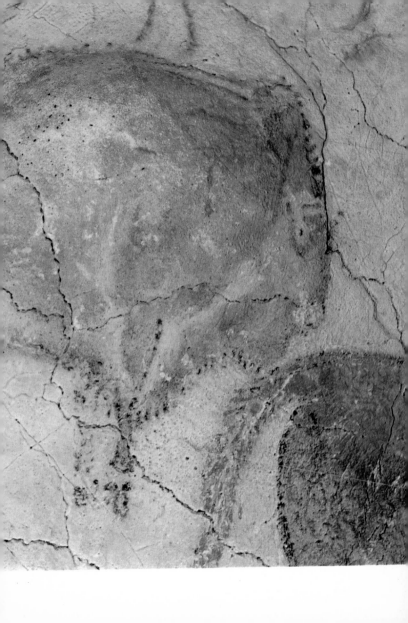

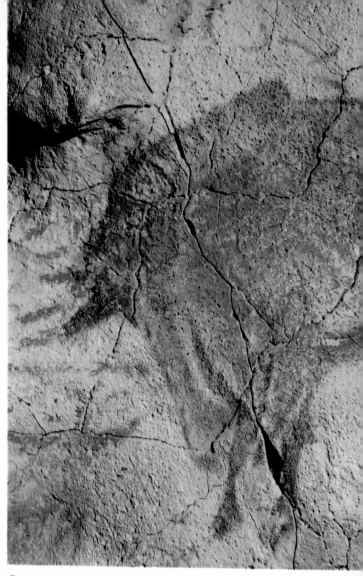

PLATES 8 AND 9

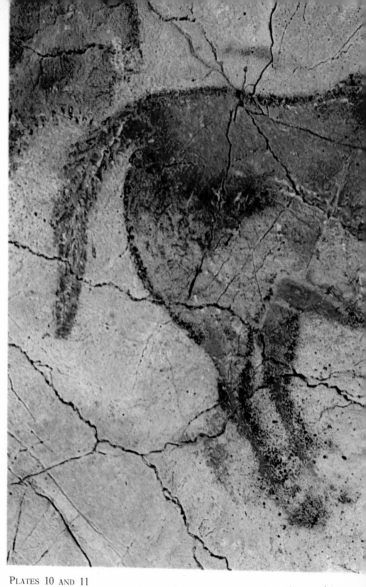

PLATES 10 AND 11

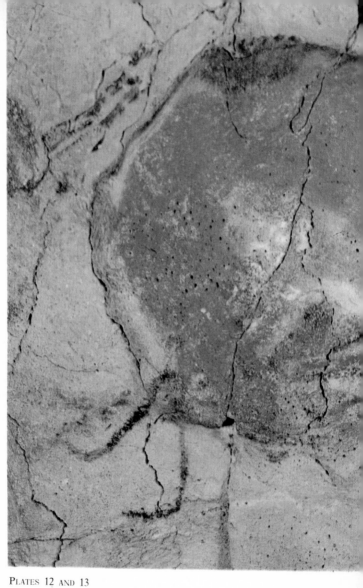

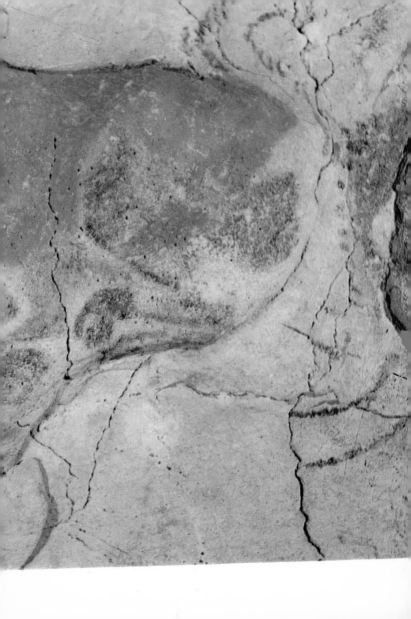

PLATES 14 AND 15

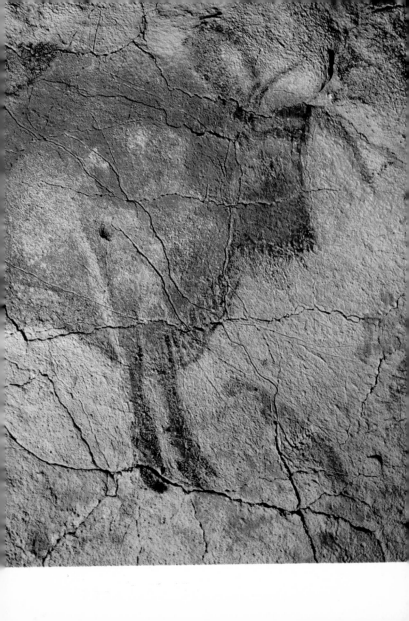

PLATE 16

PLATE 17

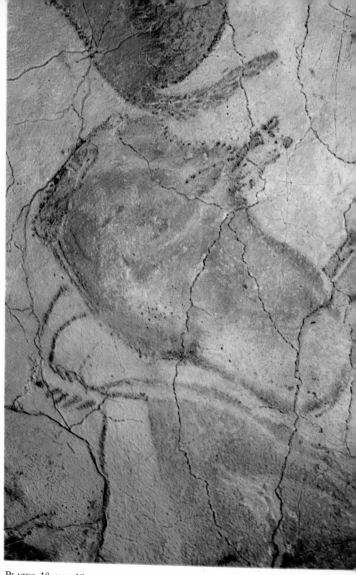

PLATES 18 AND 19

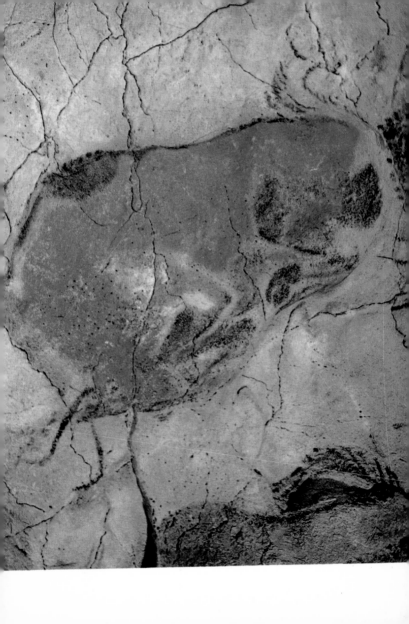

PLATES 20 AND 21

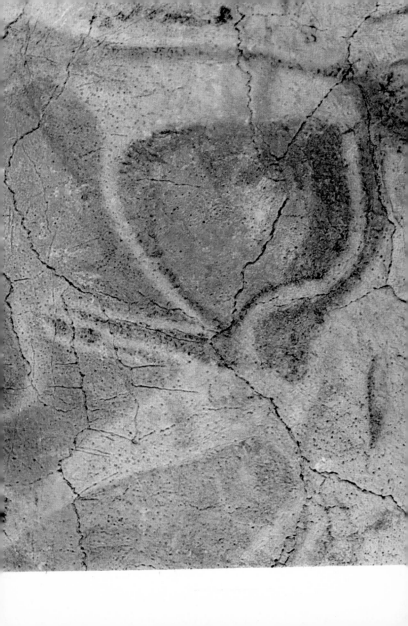

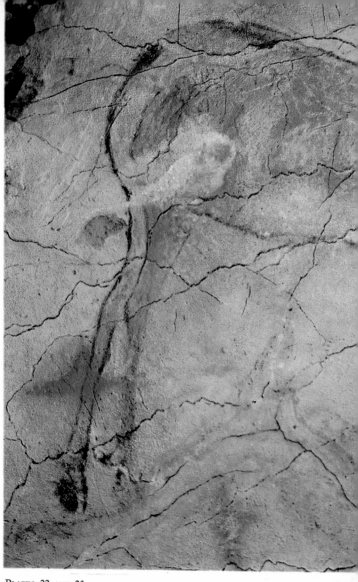

PLATES 22 AND 23

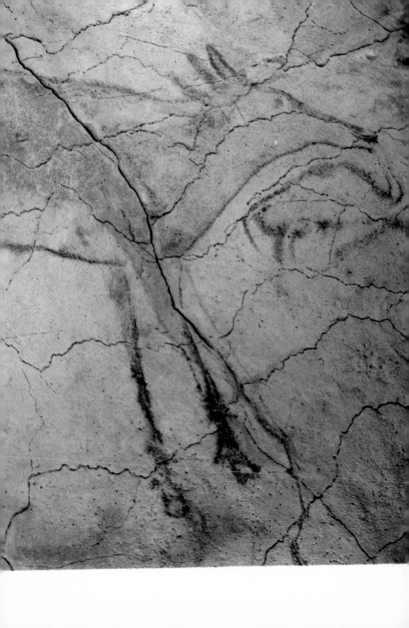

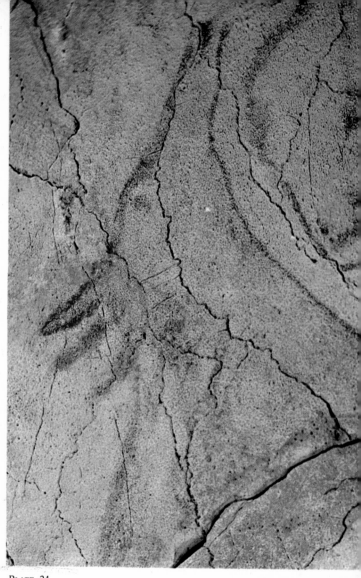

PLATE 24

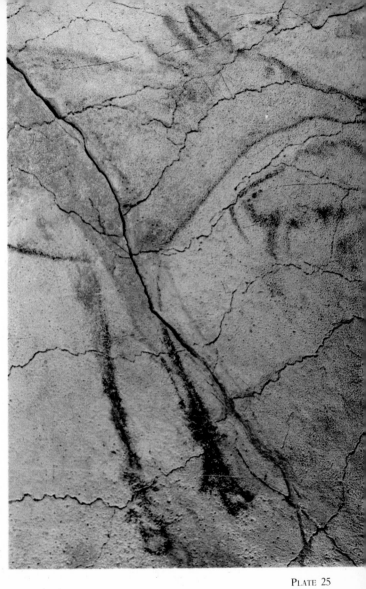

PLATE 25

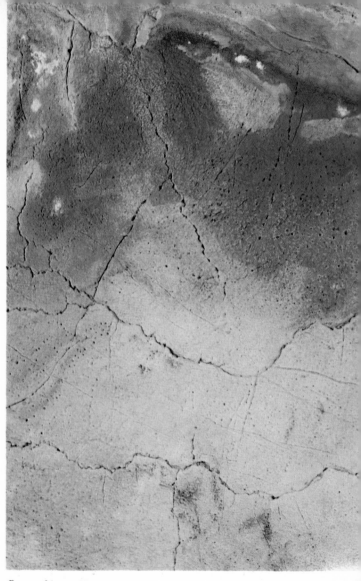

PLATES 26 AND 27

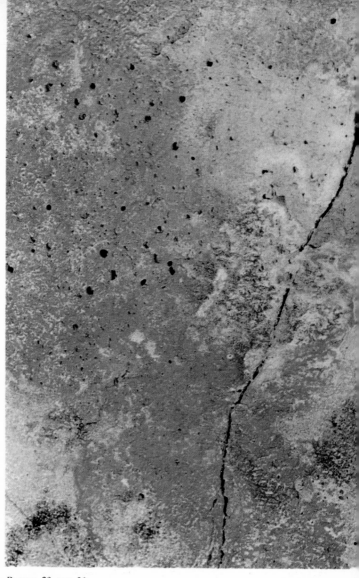

PLATES 28 AND 29

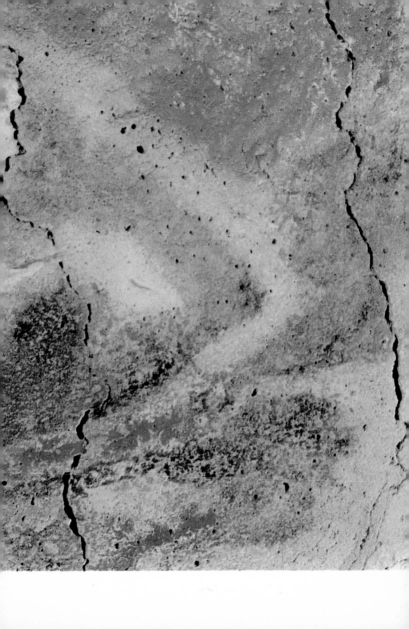

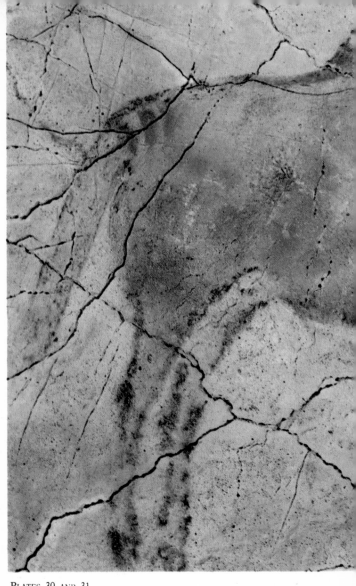

PLATES 30 AND 31

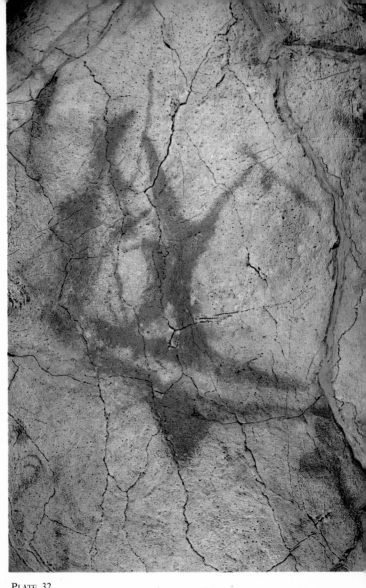

PLATE 32